Then & Now
Brentford

Then & Now
Brentford

Carolyn & Peter Hammond

TEMPUS

Frontispiece: The Vestry Hall on the corner of St Paul's Road and the Half Acre, designed by Nowell Parr and erected in 1899 (see page 37).

First published 2006

Tempus Publishing Limited
The Mill, Brimscombe Port,
Stroud, Gloucestershire, GL5 2QG
www.tempus-publishing.com

British Library Cataloguing in Publication Data.
A catalogue record for this book is available from the British Library.

ISBN 0 7524 3820 4

Origination by Tempus Publishing Limited.
Printed in Great Britain.

Contents

Brentford from Towing Path.

W 4627

Looking across the river from the Kew bank towards Brentford in the early 1900s.

Introduction

The photographs in this book span just over 100 years but show such major changes that it is sometimes difficult to recognise that the modern views are pictures of the same places. The pace of change has accelerated over the last fifty years and indeed our most recent 'old' photo (of St George's church) was taken in 2000, but what it shows has already changed and is set to change still further if the rumours that the church is scheduled for demolition are true.

Many of the older photographs in this book were taken by Fred Turner, for forty years the town's librarian, and a keen amateur photographer and local historian. We have also used a number of postcards from the early years of the twentieth century; some were produced locally, by Wakefield's who had a shop in the High Street, and by Walter Pearce whose printing works were in The Butts. However, we would not have been able to complete this book without the work of Mr R.F. Holman who worked in the planning department at the Glenhurst Road offices of the Middlesex County Council from 1950, and became the planning officer for the Borough of Hounslow in 1965. He carefully and conscientiously photographed all the buildings in the areas which were being considered for redevelopment after the end of the Second World War, and his photographs are a wonderful record of the town as it had been for decades, just before everything started to change.

At the time of the earliest photographs in this book the population of Brentford was about 15,000 and many of the people were employed in the traditional local industries, brewing, soap making, tanning, boat building and repairing, market gardening or working at the gas works, the waterworks, the fruit and vegetable market, the dock and on the canal. They lived in streets of small terraced houses built in the nineteenth century or in alleyways of old tenements. After two world wars, the Depression, the coming of the Great West Road, the closure of almost all the local industries and several comprehensive redevelopment plans, none of which were fully implemented, Brentford has now become 'Trendy TW8'. Commercial developers are taking advantage of Brentford's position on the river and canal and replacing the industrial premises of the past with monolithic blocks of modern flats.

We have arranged the photographs as a tour of the area, which we hope will make it easy for readers to find their way around the book. We start at Brentford Market and move along Kew Bridge Road and the High Street as far as the Half Acre, then turn right up the Half Acre and Boston Manor Road to Boston Manor Station. Then we pick up the route at the Half Acre and proceed along the western half of the High Street as far as Brentford Bridge. Next we take to the water from Kew Bridge, along the Thames and up the canal as far as Brentford Lock. Finally we visit to Gunnersbury Park followed by a trip along the Great West Road.

Collecting these images of Brentford in the past and comparing them with how the area looks now has been an interesting and challenging experience, and we hope that this record of Brentford past and present will encourage people to take an interest in the area's rich history and heritage.

Acknowledgements

We are most grateful for all the help we have received while compiling this book, and in particular we should like to thank the following: Gillian Clegg, the author of *Brentford Past*, an invaluable history of the area, for her interest in the project and for reading and commenting on the drafts of all the captions; Celia Cotton, the creator of a very informative website on the history of Brentford High Street (www.bhsproject.co.uk) for answering our questions and allowing us access to her unpublished research; Peter and Mary Downes for allowing us to browse through Peter's huge collection of postcards and select our favourites; transport experts John Gillham and Richard Clarke for sharing their extensive knowledge of local trains, buses and trams; the staff of Kew Bridge Steam Museum and especially Lesley Bossine, Josephine Willis and Richard Albanese for helping us find and identify images from their collection; Peter Quennell for making a special journey to bring us his great-grandfather's photograph and tell us about his family; Pam Vernon-Roberts for allowing us access to her work on the firm of E.C. Jones; Diana Willment for a guided tour of the river and canal sites and her help with the relevant captions.

We should also like to thank the following for their help while we were writing the captions and taking the modern photographs: Nadine Dunn-Meynell, Vanda Foster, Mike Galer, Phil Goldby, Eileen Henderson, Peter McDermott, Ruth Maranzi, James Marshall and Bill White.

The majority of the old photographs in this book come from the collections held at Chiswick Public Library (2, 11, 14, 15, 18, 19, 20, 21, 23, 24, 27, 28, 30, 31, 33, 34, 35, 36, 37, 38, 39, 41, 43, 44, 49, 50, 51, 52, 54, 56, 57, 58, 60, 61, 62, 64, 65, 66, 69, 70, 71, 72, 74, 75, 76, 77, 78, 90, 93, 94), Gunnersbury Park Museum (22, 55, 79, 82, 83, 84, 85, 86) and Hounslow Public Library (87, 88, 89, 91, 92, 95) and we thank the London Borough of Hounslow for permission to use them. In addition we should like to thank the staff: Catherine Taylor at Chiswick, Vanda Foster at Gunnersbury and James Marshall at Hounslow, who could not have been more helpful in allowing us access to their collections. In some cases the photographs had been copied from originals belonging to other institutions or individuals and we should like to thank the following for permission to use their pictures: John Bell 90; *Brentford, Chiswick and Isleworth Times* 72, 94; English Heritage NMR 84; Jerome Farrell 58; John Gillham 19, 36, 43, 61, 62; Paul Gorringe 15; Peter McDermott 70; Janet McNamara 39; National Motor Museum Beaulieu 83.

We are most grateful to the following for allowing us to borrow items from their collections: Peter Downes 10, 12, 13, 40, 42, 45, 46, 53, 59, 68; Grand Union Community Development 26 (by courtesy of Eileen Henderson and Paul Kyle); Kew Bridge Steam Museum 16, 17 (by courtesy of Thames Water), 63 (held in trust in the archive collection at the Museum); London's Transport Museum © Transport for London 48; Peter Quennell 47; Pam Vernon-Roberts 73.

The following items came from the authors' own collection: 6, 9, 25, 29, 32, 67, 80, 81.

In some cases it has not been possible to identify the copyright owners or to trace their current addresses, so we apologise if we have unintentionally infringed anyone's copyright.

1

Market to Ealing Road

*L*ooking across Kew Bridge towards the most easterly part of Brentford in the early 1900s. Until the 1930s this was the only road bridge across the Thames between Hammersmith and Richmond. This part of Brentford was dominated by four large employers: the wholesale fruit and vegetable market, the Grand Junction Waterworks, the gas works and the Royal Brewery.

Kew Bridge Road.

W.HA3112.

*L*ooking east along the High Road from the junction with Lionel Road in the early 1900s. In the 1880s there had been an unofficial open-air market on the north side of Kew Bridge. This led to many complaints about traffic congestion until the Brentford Local Board bought some land from the Gunnersbury Park Estate on the north side of the main road and opened the first stage of Brentford's wholesale fruit and vegetable market in 1893. The single-storey market buildings on the left enclosed an extensive courtyard where carts could be parked and there were also covered stalls for rent around the sides. On the right-hand side is the turn into Stile Hall Gardens and beyond that the tall buildings of Stile Hall Parade. These were built on the site of a large mansion called Stile Hall which fronted the main road and whose grounds stretched from Wellesley Road to the railway line. It was demolished in 1890–91. The modern view shows the new buildings on the market site and Chiswick Flyover in the distance.

This imposing façade was originally the main entrance to Brentford fruit and vegetable market after an extension was constructed in 1905. Seated griffins watch over the entrance from the pinnacles above the archway. The 1893 market had proved so successful that the council bought more land adjacent to it a few years later and an extension was designed by their architect Nowell Parr and opened in 1906. This provided a much larger covered area,

further open space for carts and more shops fronting onto the main road. This photograph was taken at around the time the market closed in 1974 when all the market traders had moved to new purpose-built premises near Southall. The buildings were later used for a

Sunday market and then a skateboarding rink before being demolished in 1982. The modern photograph shows some of the office blocks and warehouses which were built on the market's site, and on the right the Brentford Fountain Leisure Centre, opened in 1987.

*L*ooking north from the end of Kew Bridge in the early 1900s. This was the end of the route for horse-drawn trams coming from Chiswick and Shepherds Bush and remained the terminus when the tram service was first electrified in 1901. Later that year the service was extended along Kew Bridge Road and Brentford High Street to Hounslow. Behind the tram is Kew Bridge railway station, opened in 1849 on the line from Hounslow to Barnes and thence to Waterloo. The station house was designed by Sir William Tite, best known as the architect of the Royal Exchange. To the left is the Express public house which was erected in

the 1860s. The Aldington family took it over in 1882 and have owned it ever since. To the right is the side wall of the Star and Garter Hotel and in the centre is an elaborate drinking fountain which also provided drinking troughs for horses. The modern photograph shows a considerably more complicated traffic junction but with the same buildings round it apart from the drinking fountain.

Entrance to Kew Bridge.

Kew Bridge & Tram Terminus.

*L*ooking south across Kew Bridge in the early 1900s. This bridge is the third one on this site and was officially opened by King Edward VII and Queen Alexandra in May 1903. To the left is the Star and Garter Hotel, a famous old coaching inn, licensed from at least the middle of the eighteenth century and well known locally as a venue for meetings, dinners, concerts and balls. It closed as a pub in 1984 and was redeveloped as an office block while retaining its original façade. To the right is the elaborate fountain installed by the Metropolitan Drinking Fountain and Cattle Trough Association and unveiled by the Duchess of Teck in July 1877. The fountain proved something of a traffic hazard in the middle of the junction and it was moved to Western International Market in 1974. There are calls for it to be returned to Brentford. The modern photograph shows the façade of the old Star and Garter building and another view of the complicated traffic junction.

*T*he Q Theatre, shortly before it closed in 1956. The site next to the Star and Garter had been, in turn, the garden for the pub, a swimming pool, a roller skating rink, a dance hall, a cinema and a film studio until it was taken over by Jack and Beatie de Leon and opened as a theatre in 1924. It became one of London's foremost 'little theatres' and provided a venue for a variety of plays including many which transferred to the West End. Many stars who subsequently became famous made their first appearances here, such as Sir Dirk Bogarde, Joan Collins, Margaret Lockwood and Sir Anthony Quayle. The theatre closed in 1956 and the building was demolished in 1958. The modern photograph shows part of the front of the old Star and Garter and the apartment block called Rivers House which was converted from the large office block that was built on the site of the theatre in 1959. The office block was the headquarters of the Ralph M. Parsons Group from 1971 until the late 1990s.

*T*he south side of Kew Bridge Road looking east towards Kew Bridge in 1976. There were five public houses all within close proximity to Kew Bridge, 100 years ago, of which three have now gone: the Oxford and Cambridge by the riverside, which closed in 1923, the Plough, seen to the left in this picture, which was demolished in 2000, and the Star and Garter. Only the Express on the north side of the road and the Waggon and Horses, seen here, are still open. The Waggon and Horses was a Victorian pub which was rebuilt in the 1930s. The office block to the left of the photograph was built in 1959 and known as Kew Bridge House. It was demolished in 1992 and, as the modern photograph shows, the site has remained empty ever since. This is despite many attempts by developers to get planning approval to build unsuitably tall apartment blocks on the site. The Thameside Centre office development on the right in the modern photograph was opened in 1987, replacing the row of terraced houses.

*A*n aerial view of the river bank near the waterworks in the 1980s when Bangor Road and the surrounding area was being cleared for redevelopment. The Grand Junction Waterworks Company moved from a polluted site at Chelsea to Brentford in 1837 to draw water from the Thames to supply north-west London. The water was pumped from the river and onwards by huge steam-powered beam engines. The little dock inlet in the centre of the photograph was probably constructed to allow the unloading of the components of the huge pumping engines which were delivered by water. There was another small inlet a little further west where coal for the boilers that powered the pumping engines was unloaded from barges into railway trucks and transported under the road in a tunnel.

Water is still pumped from Brentford, but not taken directly from the river here. The pumping is now done by modern electric equipment, and in 1975 the historic buildings and majestic steam pumps became the Kew Bridge Steam Museum. The modern photograph shows the same view today with the Thameside Centre office complex which was completed in 1987.

A view across the filter beds and reservoirs of the waterworks looking west towards the gas works, c. 1960. Initially the water was pumped from the Thames at Brentford but by 1855 it was being piped in from Hampton and then cleaned at Brentford where the impurities were removed by allowing the water to settle through layers of sand in the filter beds. The clean water was then pumped to reservoirs for storage. The filter beds had to be cleaned regularly: the sand was raked up, moved to the cleaning area, washed in hoppers and then transported back and spread out over the filter beds again. By the 1960s the Metropolitan Water Board no longer needed such a large area and part of its land was bought by the Brentford and Chiswick Council as a site for a new housing project. The modern photograph shows two of the six tower blocks of flats built on the site of the disused filter beds. Each block is named after the type of engine, the engineers or the companies connected with the beam engines in the waterworks. In the middle distance the Holland Gardens flats have replaced the gas holders.

The north side of Kew Bridge Road, looking east, in 1900. In the distance on the right is the Grand Junction Waterworks' standpipe tower which contains the pipes originally used to maintain even water pressure in the mains. The tower was built in 1867 to replace an earlier lattice structure after the pipes had been damaged by frost. In the centre of the photograph is the Fox and Hounds pub, licensed from the middle of the eighteenth century, one of many pubs along the main road. It closed around 1919. Many of the buildings in this photograph were swept away for the expansion of the gas works in the 1920s. After the gas works closed in 1963 the site remained undeveloped until 2000 when work started

on the blocks of flats in Holland Gardens, seen on the left of the modern photograph. The road was named in memory of Frank Holland, founder of the Musical Museum in St George's church. The square building with the central tower in the middle of the modern photograph is the new home for the Musical Museum, which at the time of writing was being prepared for opening in 2007.

*B*rentford High Street, looking west, in 1962. This stretch of the High Street was dominated by the high walls and buildings of the gas works which at its peak occupied over 8 acres of land on both sides of the road. The gas works was founded in 1820 on a small riverside site, convenient for deliveries of coal by barge. Initially the gas was just used for lighting the main

roads but by the 1850s it was also being used for domestic heating and lighting. As the population grew so did the demand for gas until the works stretched for a quarter mile along the road. People would come specifically to breathe in the fumes as they were thought to be beneficial for bronchial problems. The works closed in 1963 when natural gas superseded manufactured town gas, and

demolition of the buildings started in the mid-1960s. The high wall that concealed the view of the river was eventually lowered in 1977, and after decontamination of the site, Watermans Park and the Watermans Arts Centre were opened in 1982 and 1984 respectively on the south side of the road. The area on the north side of the road was not redeveloped for the flats of Holland Gardens until 2000.

*A*n unobstructed view of St George's church in August 2000 after the buildings which had surrounded it had just been demolished. The first church on this site was built in the 1760s as a private chapel by a group of local residents and designed by John Joshua Kirby of Kew. It was consecrated as a parish church in 1828, but in due course proved too small and was demolished and rebuilt in 1886–87 to the design of A.W. Blomfield. The tower was added in 1913 as the result of a legacy from Thomas Layton, a churchwarden there, and a noted local dignitary and antiquarian. It closed as a church in 1959, and became the home of the Musical Museum founded by Frank Holland in 1963, housing a collection of mechanical musical instruments. The single-storey white painted building

beyond the church is the Sunday school for poor children founded by Mrs Sarah Trimmer, Mr Kirby's daughter, in 1786. As the modern photograph shows, the church is now surrounded again, by a recently opened Travelodge to the west and by the blocks of flats in Holland Gardens to the north and east. At the time of writing the church is empty, and its fate is uncertain.

*T*he north side of the High Street looking west towards Ealing Road in 1961. The Barge Aground was licensed by at least the early eighteenth century and was rebuilt in 1902. Just beyond the advertisement hoardings is Distillery Road, on the site of a large distillery which in the 1840s was producing nearly 1 million gallons of spirits annually. It closed in the 1850s and Distillery Road was built over its site in the 1870s. Not long after this photograph was taken this stretch of the High Street was cleared of buildings as part of the Brentford and Chiswick Council's improvement plans for the area from Ealing Road to New Road. The new houses and flats were named the Haverfield Estate after a prominent local family who owned property in this area in the nineteenth century. The first families moved into their new homes in 1973. The building in the modern photograph is the entrance to the block appropriately called Distillery Walk, preserving the memory of a vanished local industry.

Pottery Road looking south in the early 1960s. Pottery Road was built in the early 1880s, one of many streets of small terraced dwellings put up to house the workers from Brentford's many industrial concerns in the Victorian period. It was so named as it led to a large pottery established in the mid-eighteenth century which produced mainly red ware such as chimney pots and flower pots. This had closed before the First World War. The road had originally been known as Bull Lane, after the long-established pub called the Bull on the west corner of the junction with the High Street. The lower end of the street was overshadowed by the towering buildings of the gas works which dominated

the skyline. The gas works and the streets which had housed its workers were demolished at roughly the same time in the 1960s. The modern photograph shows the 1970s houses with gardens set at right angles to the line of the original road, which replaced the old terraced houses, whose front doors opened straight onto the street.

*T*he junction of the High Street with Ealing Road, looking west in 1961 and showing the old Red Lion pub on the corner. There had been a Red Lion in Old Brentford since at least the 1660s, presumably on this site. This pub was rebuilt in 1907 and demolished in 1970. The old name for Ealing Road was Drum Lane as there had been a pub on the east side of the junction called the Drum Inn since at least 1722. It had been demolished in 1921 for an earlier road-widening exercise. Up to the 1960s shops and houses lined the High Street right up to the junction with Ealing Road but the council was pursuing its policy of opening up the area, and when this photograph was taken there were already plans for widening the road and improving the road junction. The modern view shows Osier Court, built in the late 1980s on the west side of the junction, and the McDonald's fast-food outlet on the east side, which replaced the modern Red Lion pub.

Another view of the old Red Lion pub, this time looking east, just before it closed in 1965. A new Red Lion pub had been built to replace it on the opposite corner of Ealing Road prior to the closure of the old Red Lion. This is the building in the centre of the picture, photographed shortly before its opening in November 1965. The Red Lion won the *Evening Standard* Pub of the Year award in 1967 and was well known for its live music. The site was sold to McDonald's in 1996. The company pulled the pub down and replaced it with the fast-food outlet seen in the modern photograph on the previous page. Beyond the new pub the site is being cleared for redevelopment. On the right is one of the giant gas holders that overshadowed St George's church. They were not demolished until 1988. In the modern photograph Osier Court has replaced one Red Lion and McDonald's the other, and between them are the houses and flats of the Haverfield Estate.

2

High Street – East

*T*he High Street, looking west from the junction with Town Meadow in the early 1900s. This shows a typical mix of buildings of different dates and styles, houses, shops, pubs and industrial buildings. In this slightly wider section of the main road there was not such a conflict between trams and other road users as developed further west.

*L*ooking west along the High Street from the junction with Ealing Road in the early 1950s. The large building on the right is the police station, erected in 1869. At that time it was home to Inspector James Tarling and his wife and children. They shared it with eighteen police constables, three of them with their wives. The building became redundant when a new police station and section house was opened in the Half Acre in 1966, and it was demolished three years later. Next door to the police station the gap in the hoardings led to the Thames Steam Tug & Lighterage Company which was established in the nineteenth century. The company registered over eighty boats at Brentford. Its premises extended down to the river where barges were built and repaired. Some of the buildings are still there, including the sheds on Lot's Ait, although the firm closed in 1980. The modern photograph shows the site is now occupied by two large office blocks, Albany House and Thameside House. Both are empty.

*L*ooking down Ferry Lane towards the Thames in 1962. This was one of the many alleyways that led from the High Street to the wharves on the river. The principal business at the bottom of Ferry Lane was the Thames Soap Works, but there were also timber wharves and the premises of Clements Knowling & Co., barge owners and contractors. In common with many of the alleyways there was also a public house, in this case the Waterman's Arms, here since at least the middle of the eighteenth century, but rebuilt during the earlier part of the twentieth century. The little garden on the left was once the site of seven small almshouses for poor women of the parish, grouped round a tiny yard. They were

closed in 1949. As the modern photograph shows, the old buildings down the lane have been replaced by the flats of the Ferry Quays development, started in 2000, and to the left of the garden is the Premier Travel Inn which opened in September 2003.

The north side of the High Street from Number 275 to Albany Place in the 1960s, a typical stretch of Brentford High Street as it was until the major redevelopment of the second half of the twentieth century. Buildings of different dates and styles were tightly packed together and offered a wide variety of shops, including on the left Percy Goddard & Sons, 'complete house furnishers'. The shop on the extreme right with the two bay windows was Rattenbury & Co. This building had been a pawnbroker's for over a century and the three golden balls hanging outside signify it was still offering that service in the 1960s. After it closed in 1968, the shop fronts were acquired by the Museum of London and at the time of writing were on display in the Museum's Victorian Shop Fronts section. The modern view shows the flats of Watermans Court, which were built in the early 1990s.

*T*he High Street, looking east, in the early 1900s. The large building on the right is the fire station, built in 1897 to the design of Nowell Parr, Brentford Council's architect. It had a 'commodious engine room' for two appliances, a three-storey open tower for drying the leather hoses, and a yard for drilling. The horses were stabled nearby as Brentford did not acquire a motor fire engine until 1924. The fire station closed in 1965; it was used by the ambulance service for the next twenty years, then converted into offices, and finally opened as a restaurant in 2003. Beyond the fire station the small building with the tall chimneys housed three of the group of seven small almshouses mentioned on page twenty-seven. The modern view shows that the premises of Young & Marten, builders' merchants, have given way to the Premier Travel Inn and on the opposite side of the road the sweep of shops has been replaced by the flats of Watermans Court.

*T*he north side of the High Street just east of the garden of the block of flats called Berkeley House, seen in the 1970s. This unusual little building opened as the Brentford Cinema in 1912. It was renamed the Coronet Cinema after renovations in 1923 but could not compete with the larger cinemas which were installing sound equipment for showing talking pictures in the late 1920s, and it closed around 1930. The premises then became a garage and later the electro-plating workshop of the Press Plating Company. The building

was finally demolished in the 1980s. The clue to the location of this building is the block of flats showing over the rooftop. This is Berkeley House, built in the early 1960s, replacing a row of small shops and houses. The alleyway which skirts the east side of the garden of Berkeley House used to be called Kings Arms Alley, a reminder of the Kings Arms pub which stood on that corner in the nineteenth century.

*T*he north side of the High Street, just east of the Half Acre, in the late 1960s when the area was being cleared for redevelopment. The neglected building in the centre is the Wesleyan Methodist chapel off St Paul's Road which was opened in 1864. It had a gallery all round inside and could seat 400 people. After the new Methodist church was built on the corner of Windmill and Clifden Roads in 1889 it was only used for Sunday schools and later as church offices. It functioned as the Middlesex County Council's Technical Education Polytechnic for five years from the late 1890s and then became an organ factory until the 1920s. Finally, it was used for light engineering and as a warehouse and was eventually demolished in 1977. In the background can be seen the tall block of the police section house opened in 1966 and the spire of St Paul's church half hidden behind the side wall of the flats called St Paul's House. Once the site had been cleared it became the car park for Brentford's first supermarket, International Stores, which opened in 1983. This later became Gateway and has been Somerfield since 1992.

*S*t Paul's church seen from the south east in the early 1900s. St George's was the original parish church for Old Brentford, the eastern half of Brentford, but by the middle of the nineteenth century it was too small and too inconveniently sited to serve the whole parish so a new church, seating 700, was built in 1867–68. It was designed in early decorated style by Horace and Frederick John Francis and built in Kentish ragstone. The spire was completed in 1869 and can be seen from many parts of Brentford. In 1961, after the closure of St George's and of St Lawrence's (the

parish church for the western part of Brentford) St Paul's became the principal church of the United Parish of Brentford.

In the early 1990s St Paul's was altered and enlarged to the design of the architect Michael Blee. He created a new parish church and community centre at a cost of £4 million, which was raised from the sale of the redundant church of St James' Gunnersbury. The architect retained the spire and the south wall of the original building and created a new polygonal church area on the north side of the nave. The raised chancel became a side chapel, and the nave and a new hall on the north side provide spaces for community activities. The renovated building, shown in the modern photograph, won awards from the Civic Trust and the RIBA.

*T*he south side of the High Street, looking west towards Catherine Wheel Road, in the early 1950s. The house on the left was built in the eighteenth century and is now a listed building. During the nineteenth century it was successively home to two prosperous local families. The house was later divided into flats and in 1999 it was refurbished and is now offices. The house next door is also eighteenth century but has been considerably altered.

The building on the right was the premises of the London Radio College which was set up in the 1920s to train radio operators for the merchant navy. The college moved to Chiswick in the mid-1930s and closed in the late 1950s. The modern view shows that the building of the London Radio College has been replaced by the premises of Wilson & Kyle. This was a precision engineering company set up in Catherine Wheel Yard in the 1920s. It moved into new premises here in the mid-1950s but closed in 1998.

The High Street, looking east from the junction with the Half Acre, in 1899. The road was being dug up to lay the tramlines for the new electric tram service to Hounslow, inaugurated in 1901. The steel rails were laid on a layer of concrete 6in below the road surface and the surface was then levelled with wood blocks waterproofed with creosote and tar. The butcher's shop was originally the building on the corner of the Half Acre and the Beehive pub was two doors further east. However, when the Half Acre was widened in 1905 to take the tram service up to Hanwell the building line was moved back and most of the shops and cottages lining the road were demolished. The Beehive then became the corner building and was rebuilt to the design of Brentford Council's architect, Nowell Parr. When he wasn't designing municipal buildings he had a small private practice specialising in pub architecture. The modern photograph shows the Beehive pub on one corner and the 1950s premises of Wilson & Kyle on the other.

3

Half Acre to Boston Manor

*B*oston Manor House in the 1950s. The house was built in the early seventeenth century and became the home of the Clitherow family, Lords of the Manor of Boston for 250 years. The route up the Half Acre to Boston Manor marked the boundary between the parishes of New Brentford to the west and Old Brentford to the east.

*L*ooking north up the Half Acre in November 1960, not long before the overhead wires were removed and the trolley buses replaced by motor buses. The road had originally been much narrower, with some buildings dating back to the seventeenth and eighteenth centuries, although by 1905 the old cottages and little shops were shabby and dilapidated. Many of these had to be demolished to widen the road sufficiently to establish an electric tram service up the Half Acre and Boston Manor Road to Hanwell. The

service started in 1906, and thirty years later trolley buses took over from trams. The service is still in operation today; the route is now served by E8 single-decker buses. Only a few years after this photograph was taken the road was redeveloped once again and, as the modern picture shows, most of the buildings have been demolished, with the notable exception of the Beehive pub on the right-hand side at the corner with the High Street.

*T*wo of the landmark buildings in the Half Acre being demolished in 1963. In the centre is the shell of the Queens Cinema. It had opened before the First World War and could seat 600 people. It outlived the other local cinemas but closed down suddenly in December 1957; the owners said it was running at a loss. In the distance on the left are the remains of one of Brentford's most striking buildings, the

Vestry Hall on the corner of St Paul's Road (see frontispiece). This was built in 1899 by the Overseers of the Poor and designed by Brentford Council's architect, Nowell Parr. It contained a large hall seating 600, with a stage, two committee rooms, offices for the Collectors of the Poor Rate and a soup kitchen in the basement. In 1907 the County Court moved there from the Town Hall and remained until a new court house in Alexandra Road was opened in 1963. The building was then pulled down, despite a campaign to save it. The modern photograph shows the police station and Section House, opened in 1966, which replaced these two buildings.

*T*he old post office building on the corner of St Paul's Road and the Half Acre in 1960. The main post office for the area moved here in 1908 from its previous location on the east side of the Market Place. In the early 1900s it was open from 7 a.m. until 10 p.m. on weekdays and from 8 a.m. until 10 a.m. on Sunday mornings. There were seven deliveries of mail every day except Sunday. The post office remained in St Paul's Road until 1960 when a new modern building was provided for it in the redeveloped section of the High Street, just east of the Market Place, not far from its original home. As the modern photograph shows, the site of the post office building is now a car park with a clearer view of the buildings in the Half Acre – the tall building in the centre is the former St Lawrence's Church of England primary school rebuilt in 1893 and closed in 1931. It is still used for educational purposes as the premises of the Brentford Day Nursery.

*T*he chapel in Boston Manor Road in 1992. This is the oldest surviving non-conformist chapel in Brentford. It was built in 1783 by the Society of Protestant Dissenters, had become a Congregational church by the middle of the nineteenth century, and became a United Reformed church in 1972 when the Congregationalists joined with the Presbyterians.

The church hall next door was built in 1871 over the top of the church's disused graveyard, and enlarged in 1906. The church originally had two storeys below roof level but it was badly damaged by a flying bomb in 1944 and restored with only one storey, so this 1992 photograph shows it as it appeared for the last fifty years of the twentieth century. In 1988 the congregation of Park Baptist chapel came to share the church buildings. The sale of their site on the Great West Road enabled the two congregations to finance the restoration of the 1783 building to its original appearance and create more meeting rooms. They also demolished the Victorian church hall and built a new chapel on its site. The work was completed in 2000, and the building is now known as Brentford Free church.

*B*oston Manor Road showing Clifden House and Brentford Library in the early 1900s. The building on the left is Clifden House, built in the mid-eighteenth century. It took its name from Henry Viscount Clifden who lived there in 1799. In 1888 it was taken over for offices by the Brentford Local Board and then by its successor, the Brentford Urban District Council. In 1927 Brentford amalgamated with Chiswick and the administrative centre of the new local authority moved to Chiswick. Clifden House continued to be used for official and local authority purposes and was eventually demolished in 1953. Next to Clifden House is the newly built public library, opened in 1904. Brentford's first library service had started in one room in Clifden House in 1890 but soon ran out of space. The solution was provided by a generous donation of £5,400 from Andrew Carnegie, the Scottish/American businessman and philanthropist. He paid for the building on condition that Brentford Council provided the site and the books. The building was designed by Nowell Parr and opened by Carnegie himself in May 1904. The modern photograph shows the library now has a larger garden which includes the War Memorial column, unveiled in 1923.

*T*he reference room in the new public library in the early 1900s. Fred Turner, the librarian who had set up the library service in Brentford in 1890 and continued to run it until his retirement in 1930, was a keen photographer, and this is one of his photographs of the interior of the new library. This view shows the reference room which was on the left-hand side of the entrance hall, with access via a doorway at the front of the hall. At this date most of the reference books were kept behind glass and the books for borrowing were stored on closely packed bookshelves out of reach of the public. Readers had to choose a title from a catalogue and then ask the librarian to fetch it for them. The public were not allowed to have free access to browse among the books until 1923. However, the opening hours were more generous than current hours – initially the library was open from 9 a.m. until 10 p.m. every day except Sunday. The modern photograph shows that the reference room has become the children's library and the counter with a window above, from which the librarian could supervise the readers, has become the entrance to the room.

*T*he Methodist church on the corner of Windmill and Clifden Roads in the early 1900s. The Methodist church was opened in 1890. It was built in an ornate Gothic style in contrast to the classical chapel in St Paul's Road which it replaced. (See Page 31). It had a spacious and lofty interior with a deep gallery round three sides and could seat 1,100 people. The spire was added in 1903. In 1961 the congregations from the Methodist churches in Clifden Road and New Road joined together and the Clifden Road church and the church hall next to it were demolished. A new, smaller church incorporating some stained glass from the earlier church was built on the eastern part of the site where the church hall had been and opened in 1964. The modern photograph shows Clifden House, the block of flats which was built on the site of the church itself. Note the change in style of the street lighting.

Wesleyan Chapel, Brentford. W7581

*B*rentford Central Station in 1961. The station was opened in 1849 as Brentford Station but was renamed Brentford Central in 1950. It was on the newly built London & South Western railway line from Hounslow to Barnes which linked to the existing line up to Waterloo. There was also a station at Kew Bridge to serve the eastern end of the area. The two-storey building on the right of the photograph would have been the station master's house and the single-storey building on the left housed the booking hall and waiting room. The station has been altered and extended over the years, most recently in 2002 in a £2.5 million joint project between GlaxoSmithKline, the London Borough of Hounslow and Railtrack. The modern photograph shows the remodelled booking hall and the building on the left which houses a new footbridge and passenger lifts.

*B*rentford Hospital, Boston Manor Road, photographed for the opening brochure in 1928. Brentford's first hospital had been set up in Marlborough House in The Butts in 1893 with only six beds and accommodation for nurses who visited patients in their own homes. This new purpose-built hospital opened in May 1928 after a long fundraising campaign. It provided seventeen beds plus four cots for babies, staff accommodation, an operating theatre and an out-patients' department. Despite public protests it was closed in 1977, and the building became an old people's home. The residents were moved out in 1993 and the building was then demolished. It was replaced by the Health Centre, shown in the modern photograph, which opened in 1996 and provides a base for the local general practitioners and ancillary services. There is also a separate building, Brentford Lodge, providing respite care.

BOSTON Rᴰ BRENTFORD

*B*oston Road, later known as Boston Manor Road, looking north from near the junction with Boston Park Road, *c.* 1905. When this photograph was taken Boston Road was a wide, tree-lined road with the land belonging to Boston Manor House on the left and large old houses on the right, such as the eighteenth-century houses seen here. The traction poles to take the wires for the electric tram service to Hanwell had just been erected but the steel rails do not seem to have been laid in the road surface yet. The service started in May 1906. The modern photograph shows a less tranquil scene: Number 67, the tall building on the right, now called Prospect House, and the buildings next to it, have survived since they are protected by having been given Listed Building status but above them runs the viaduct of the M4, opened in 1965. Part of the motorway's girders can be seen along the top edge of the photograph.

The Colonel's Drive, a turning off Boston Manor Road opposite the grounds of Boston Manor House, in the early 1900s. At the time this postcard was printed the Colonel's Drive, now known as The Ride, was a gated country lane running between Boston Manor Road and Windmill Road. The only buildings in the lane at that date were Little Boston on the north side, the dower house for the Clitherow family, and Boston Lodge on the south side, both at the Windmill Road end of the lane. The most famous resident of Little Boston was John Quincy Adams, who later became the sixth President of America. He and his family rented the house from the Clitherows while he was American Minister in London in 1815–17. The colonel of the title may have been Col. James Clitherow who inherited Boston Manor House in 1805 and died in 1841 or Col. Edward John Stracey-Clitherow who inherited in 1856 and died in 1900. The Clitherows sold their estate to the Brentford Council in the early 1920s and from that time onwards more houses were built in the road.

W.H.A. 379.   Colonels Drive, Brentford.

*T*he Lodge at the entrance gates of Boston Manor House, *c.* 1905. Walter Quennell, one of the gardeners, is standing in front of the Lodge where he lived with his wife Flora and their three young children. Boston Manor House was built in the 1620s and bought by James Clitherow, a City merchant and banker, in 1670. It remained the home of generations of the Clitherow family for the next 250 years. The last descendant of the family sold the house and its grounds to Brentford Urban District Council in 1923, and the gardens were opened as a public park in 1924. The house is a fine example of Jacobean domestic architecture and is open to the public on Saturday and Sunday afternoons from Easter to October. The Lodge disappeared in the 1960s and was replaced by the less attractive house seen in the modern photograph. The handsome entrance gates with piers topped with the lion crest of the Clitherow family have also lost some of their embellishments.

*B*oston Manor Station in 1916. The station was opened in 1883, as part of the District Line service to Hounslow. It was originally called Boston Road Station but was renamed Boston Manor in 1911, although the part of Boston Road south of the station was not renamed Boston Manor Road until the 1930s. The Piccadilly Line along the same route was opened in 1933 and many of the stations were rebuilt in the period from 1931 to 1934. The modern photograph shows the new Boston Manor Station, opened in 1934. It was designed by Charles Holden, and with its distinctive tower is a characteristic example of his Modern Movement designs for the London Underground system. However, some traces of the earlier station remain, in particular the cast-iron balustrades on the stairs to the platforms and the decorative columns supporting the platform canopies. The station was protected by being given Grade II Listed Building status in March 2002.

4

High Street – West

Brentford High Street,
June 30th, 1909.

Photo. Wakefield, Brentford and Chiswick.

*B*rentford High Street looking east from the front of the Castle Hotel in 1909. The High Street was notorious for its traffic jams. The problems caused by the narrowness of the road were aggravated by the coming of the trams in 1901 and led to the building of the Great West Road after the First World War as a bypass for the High Street.

*T*he north side of the High Street at the junction with the Half Acre in the 1950s. This photograph shows the variety of architectural styles before the uniformity of the 1960s redevelopment. Some of the businesses shown here moved to new premises as the High Street was rebuilt and others just disappeared. Barclays Bank, which had been on the corner of the Half Acre since about 1900, moved to a new building on the corner of the Market Place in 1965. The building with the two triangular gables was the local branch of David Greig, the high-class grocery chain, which first opened a branch in the High Street in the 1920s, and moved to new premises at Number 205 in the 1960s. It closed in the

early 1970s. The modern photograph shows Roman House, the furniture store of Percy Goddard & Sons, which opened in 1970 on the corner site. Samuel Goddard first set up in business in Brentford in 1815 and since then members of the family have been running removal firms, estate agencies and shops selling furniture, toys, china and glass in the Brentford area.

*T*he corner of Catherine Wheel Yard (now Road) and the High Street in the early 1900s. At that date the only way into Catherine Wheel Yard was through the passageway under the building seen on the extreme left of the old photograph. To the right of the passageway was an old beer house called the Barley Corn which closed in 1908. It had belonged to Sich's Lamb Brewery of Chiswick. The brick building to the right of the two small shops housed the premises of the London and County Bank, which had moved here in the 1870s from a site near the Town Hall, on the other side of the High Street. In the 1920s part of Catherine Wheel Yard was redeveloped

and a proper road entrance was made from the High Street. The bank was rebuilt at that time; by then it was known as the Westminster Bank. The modern photograph shows that there was a further round of redevelopment in the 1950s when the shop on the corner was built, but the bank is still there, now known as the NatWest Bank.

*T*he south side of the High Street, looking west from Number 107, in the early 1950s. The shops from Number 111 as far as the Magpie and Crown pub have been pulled down and are being replaced by County Parade, a row of shops with residential accommodation above. The large building on the left with the pointed gable is the premises of James Bradbury & Son, wholesale grocers. The business was established by Thomas Bradbury at Number 108 in the 1840s, and by the 1890s it had expanded into Number 109 as well. The archway led to an extensive yard with stabling, storage areas and sheds for curing hams and smoking bacon. At the turn of the century Bradbury's ran a fleet of twenty horse-drawn

vans delivering groceries to shops within a radius of twenty miles. The firm closed in the 1960s. The modern photograph shows that Bradbury's premises has now become two shops again, and the building next door has had its roofline altered to match that of its neighbour. In the distance on the right the flats of the Brentford Lock development have replaced a row of old shops.

PETTY SESSIONAL COURT & COUNTY COURT.

*T*he Magistrates' Court in the Market Place in the early 1900s. This building was erected in 1850 by a private company, the Town Hall & Market House Company. It replaced the old market hall which had served the weekly market held here since the fourteenth century. It was never used as an official town hall but the Local Board and the Board of Guardians (predecessors of the local council) met here until they had their own premises at Clifden House and the Vestry Hall, respectively. The County Court and the Magistrates' Court were held

here, and it also housed a library and reading room, a savings bank and rooms that could be hired for meetings. In 1891 the building was purchased by the Middlesex County Council to be used as a full-time Magistrates' Court. In 1929 it was closed for two years while a new stone-faced front extension was added, as

shown in the modern photograph. The clock on the little tower on the roof was originally installed on the old market hall in 1755 by John Jullion, a celebrated local clockmaker. It was transferred to the new building in 1850 and then moved again in 1929. It is still working but is no longer wound by hand.

*T*he west side of the Market Place in the early 1950s, shortly before demolition. The building on the left and the centre with the wide arches over its ground floor windows had been the Three Pigeons pub. This was an old coaching inn which dated back to at least the fifteenth century. It was rebuilt in the nineteenth century but ceased to be a pub in 1915. Originally its stabling stretched right back to the River Brent and had room for coaches, seventy horses, and accommodation for ostlers. Before the Town Hall was built it was one of the main venues for meetings, both public and private, and hosted sessions of the Magistrates' Court and the Manorial Court. The three-storey building on the right with the arch over the top central window was run by Frank, another member of the Goddard family, as a china and glass shop, in the early 1900s. The modern photograph shows the Market Building, which replaced the old buildings on this site in the late 1950s, now home to the London Tile Company, with office accommodation above.

*T*he alleyway through from The Butts Estate to the back of the Market Place in the early 1900s. The children called the gate across the alleyway the 'penny, halfpenny and farthing' gate because of the three metal rings of different sizes that supported the cross bar; only the skinniest could crawl through the smallest 'farthing' ring and any child who could only crawl through the 'penny' was teased as a fatty. The gate disappeared after the Second World War. The Butts is a quiet enclave of late seventeenth- and early eighteenth-century houses grouped round an open space. Its name may originate in the medieval requirement for archery butts to be set up in towns so that all able-bodied men could practise using the long bow. The modern photograph shows that the house on the left of the alleyway is still there, but the old cottages are long gone although the area they occupied is still enclosed by an old wall.

The south side of The Butts showing the printing works at Number 38 in the 1950s. Walter Pearce set up a printing firm at Number 14 The Butts in around 1902 and moved to Number 38 a few years later. The business, which he called the St George's Press, expanded and prospered. In 1940 it was joined by the Buckley Press which moved out of the City of London to escape the Blitz. The businesses closed in the 1980s and, as the modern photograph shows, a development of Georgian-style town houses was built on the site. The development is named Caxton Mews after William Caxton, England's first printer. The open space in the middle of The Butts Estate was not always as tranquil as shown in these photographs, since it was the polling place for the sometimes rowdy elections of the members of parliament for the County of Middlesex during the eighteenth and nineteenth centuries.

*B*radshaw's Yard at the rear of Numbers 118 to 119 High Street in the 1950s. Thomas Bradshaw took over an existing bakery on this site in the middle of the nineteenth century and continued in business here until about 1900. The bakery was succeeded

by T. Bradshaw, corn merchant, who remained here until the First World War. The premises included a yard running down to a wharf where sacks of corn or flour could be unloaded from barges. This yard was probably very similar to those behind many properties in Brentford High Street; old maps of the area show many properties with narrow frontages but behind them long alleyways and yards leading to extensive runs of outbuildings, workshops and tenements. Those south of the High Street often had yards leading down to wharves on the edge of the canal or river. The modern view shows County Parade from the rear; the planners evidently decided to retain the line of the alleyway in exactly the same position, as it is just possible to see the east wall of the Town Hall through the entrance to the alleyway in both photographs.

*T*he interior of St Lawrence's church, looking towards the altar, in the early 1900s. The nave and chancel were rebuilt in the 1760s by Thomas Hardwick, a local architect and builder, incorporating the tower which had been part of the medieval church on the same site. When the church was rebuilt it had galleries round three sides below the upper windows and was furnished with high box pews. However, when it was modernised during the Victorian period the galleries were removed, the pews replaced and Gothic-style arcades with slender wooden columns were inserted. The church was closed for worship in 1961 and since then there have been several schemes to renovate it and reopen it as a theatre or a restaurant. At the time of writing none had succeeded. The modern photograph was taken in 2002 when a few members of the local history society were allowed to visit the church. It shows a sorry picture of neglect and disrepair. The east window is boarded up and the monuments that were round the walls of the chancel have disappeared.

High Street, Brentford. No. 3550.

*T*he south side of the High Street, looking east towards St Lawrence's church, in the early 1900s. The tower of the church can be seen above a large three-storey, flat-fronted building which was a lodging house for workmen for the first half of the twentieth century, providing ninety-two beds for working men in three blocks behind the High Street façade. The pub on the right-hand side is the Six Bells, which has been on this site since at least the early eighteenth century. It was rebuilt or perhaps just re-fronted in 1904. Its name may come from the fact that St Lawrence's tower contained a peal of six bells. During the nineteenth century the short stretch of the High Street from the church to the bridge contained two other public houses, the Magnet and the Lord Nelson, on the south side, plus three more on the north side. The modern view shows that all the buildings between the church and the pub have been demolished to make way for Augustus Close, the access road for the Brentford Dock development. The pub, however, still survives, and is well known for the prowess of its darts players.

*T*he north side of the High Street and the corner of the road leading to Durham Wharf, just east of Brentford Bridge, in the 1950s. The road led down to the edge of the canal basin, formerly timber wharves and the premises of barge owners and a large tannery. In January 1841 this was the scene of a disastrous flood. Days of freezing weather followed by heavy rain and a sudden thaw caused a huge amount of flood water to pour down the canal and the River Brent, overflowing the canal basin and pouring

down this road and other alleyways taking the shortest route across the High Street and down to the Ham. The modern photograph shows a very different scene: the access route to Durham Wharf has been retained as the gap between two blocks of flats in the Brentford Lock development. The steps lead to a piazza which, it is proposed, will eventually be lined with shops and restaurants overlooking the canal basin.

*L*ooking west from Brentford Bridge along the London Road in 1962. The railway bridge carried the Great Western Railway's branch line from Southall to Brentford Dock, opened in 1859. The entrance to Brentford Town Station is just out of sight behind the embankment on the right. The line was closed for passengers in 1942, but freight was carried up to 1964 when the Dock eventually closed due to declining traffic. The bridge was dismantled in 1966 and the buildings on the left beyond the bridge were demolished to make way for Hounslow Council's Brent Lea housing development. The Northumberland Arms public house, named after the Dukes of Northumberland, the owners of Syon House, has been on this site since at least the middle of the nineteenth century. In the 1990s the pub was renamed Mary O'Riordan's. At the time of writing it was called O'Brien's.

*T*he site of Brentford Town Station, looking east towards Brentford Bridge in 1958. The single-storey shack below the advertising hoarding is all that remains of the entrance to the station on the Great Western Railway's branch line to Brentford Dock. From the entrance, steps led up to the rather exposed platforms on top of the embankment. The branch line from Southall was opened for freight in 1859 and started running passenger trains as well from 1860. Brentford was an excellent shopping centre in the late nineteenth century and passengers would travel by train to do their shopping in the great variety of shops along the High Street. The passenger service was continued up to 1942, apart from a break in the service between 1915 and 1920. The line continued to be used for freight until it closed in 1964. The modern photograph shows that the railway bridge has gone, and beyond the embankment the Holiday Inn, opened in 2005, has replaced the industrial buildings overlooking the west side of the canal basin.

5

River and Canal

*I*n the past the Thames was a busy commercial thoroughfare for transporting raw materials and manufactured goods, but it was also used for leisure pursuits. This late nineteenth-century photograph shows two paddle steamers full of visitors near Kew Bridge. Kew Pier was a regular stop for river cruises from the centre of London out to Richmond and beyond.

*K*ew Bridge being demolished, *c.* 1899. This was the second bridge on this site, replacing a wooden bridge which had only lasted thirty years. It was opened in 1789 and was built of stone to a design by James Paine, who also designed the existing Richmond Bridge. By the 1890s Kew Bridge's steep gradient, narrow carriageway and general deterioration were giving cause for concern and it was agreed that a new bridge should be built at a cost of around £250,000 to be paid for in equal parts by the County Councils of Middlesex and Surrey. Before demolition started in 1899, a temporary wooden bridge,

partly visible through the arches, was erected on the upstream side of the bridge to take the traffic while the bridge was being rebuilt. The new bridge was officially opened by King Edward VII and Queen Alexandra in May 1903. The modern photograph shows the third or, to give it its official title, the 'King Edward VII' bridge, with local landmark, the standpipe tower of the waterworks in the distance.

*L*ooking west from Kew Bridge towards Brentford Ait in the 1950s. In the eighteenth century there was a pub on the Ait called the Three Swans with a reputation for cooked eels and rowdy drinkers. Early in the nineteenth century the island was bought by a Kew resident, the offending pub was closed down and the island was planted with trees to protect Kew from the 'inferior buildings of Brentford'. Despite its name, the Ait is in Surrey, not Middlesex, and comes under the control of the London Borough of Richmond. Until recently this part of the riverside was entirely industrial with boat-building sheds, the gas works and a timber wharf, with the skyline dominated by a huge gas holder. Now the highest buildings are the modern flats of Holland Gardens replacing the gas board's premises on the north side of the High Street, while the gas works on the south side with its high wall has given place to the open space of Watermans Park, opened in 1982. Mooring posts along the river bank with metal tops inscribed with the initials of the 'Gas Light and Coke Company' are clues to the site's industrial past.

The premises of the Royal Brewery seen from Brentford Ait in the early 1900s. There was a brewery on this site since at least the early eighteenth century, when it was known as the British Brewery. It changed its name to the Red Lion Brewery in 1825. In 1829 Felix Booth, the chairman, contributed £17,000 towards the cost of an expedition to discover the North West Passage from the Atlantic to the Pacific Oceans and in gratitude King William IV allowed him to rename the brewery the Royal Brewery, and later made him a baronet. Sir Felix also owned a large distillery on the north side of the High Street, and was the first chairman of the Brentford Gas Company in 1821. In 1922 the brewery and its 102 pubs and off-licences were bought by Style & Winch and brewing on this site ceased the following year. The buildings were swallowed up by the expansion of the gas works. The modern photograph was taken from the Kew bank looking across the Ait, and shows the Watermans Arts Centre, opened in 1984, which now occupies the brewery site.

Brentford Ferry.

Brentford ferry seen from the Kew bank in the early 1900s when Arthur East was landlord of the Ferry Hotel. For many centuries a ferry had operated from the bottom of Ferry Lane across to Kew, but it closed in 1939 and never restarted after the Second World War. The Ferry Hotel was built around 1880 to replace an earlier pub called the Bunch of Grapes. It ceased to be a pub in 1922, and was used as offices by Clements, Knowling & Co. which by then was the lessee of the ferry. The pub was demolished in 1983. On the edge of the landing stage, just to the left of the pub's notice board, is the site where the Monument (see next page) was to be erected in 1909, probably not long after this photograph was taken. To the left of that are the extensive premises of T.B. Rowe's Thames Soap Works, established in Brentford in 1799, with the Georgian house, home of the Rowe family (see page 70), in the centre. The modern photograph shows the blocks of flats of the Ferry Quays development, started in 2000, with the Georgian house surviving incongruously in the middle.

The Brentford Monument, soon after it was unveiled on Ferry Wharf in 1909. The Monument commemorates four episodes in the history of Brentford: Julius Caesar's supposed crossing of the Thames here around 54 BC; King Offa's Church Council at Brentford in AD 780-81; Canute being driven across the Thames by Edmund Ironside in AD 1016; the Battle of Brentford between the Royalists and the Parliamentarians in AD 1642. The granite cylinders had originally supported the lights on Brentford Bridge and when the bridge was widened in 1909 they were no longer required so were used to construct the Monument – an early example of recycling. The Monument was the brainchild of Sir Montagu Sharpe, the noted local antiquarian, and it must have been a proud moment as he watched its unveiling by His Grace the Duke of Northumberland from Syon House on 12 May 1909. Now on the site is a piece of modern art by Simon Packard entitled 'Liquidity'. It was unveiled in September 2003 and is made of electro-polished stainless steel plates, laser cut with images of local wildlife.

*T*he Brentford Monument in 1983. The Monument's original site on the edge of Ferry Wharf did not prove an ideal location, and by the 1950s it was neglected and forgotten among coal heaps and other material stored on the wharf. Varley Pumps & Engineering, which by then was occupying the old Thames Soap Works site, undertook to rescue the Monument. The firm repaired it, had its lettering re-cut and made a special inlet in their boundary wall to house it. It was unveiled in its new site on the west side of Ferry Lane in April 1955. Unfortunately, during the renovations it lost part of its plinth and the two cylinders were rotated so that the lower half commemorating the unveiling of the Monument is no longer paired with Edmund Ironside's victory over the Danes in 1016. In 1992 it was moved again, to a more prominent site, to mark the 350th anniversary of the Battle of Brentford, when the town was sacked by Royalist troops during the Civil War. The modern photograph shows the Monument in its new home in front of the County Court on the corner of the High Street and Alexandra Road. This building was opened by the Lord Chancellor in January 1963 to replace the unsatisfactory court premises in the Vestry Hall. The carving of the Royal Arms on the wall was designed by James Woodford, who also designed the statues of the Queen's Beasts in Kew Gardens.

*T*he premises of the Peerless Pump Company seen from the river front, *c.* 1982. The large house to the right, surrounded by the factory premises, dates back to the 1720s. It was originally a pair of semi-detached houses, one fronting onto Ferry Lane and the other looking the opposite way. They were bought by the Rowe family, the owners of the Thames Soap Works, in 1806, and the right-hand half became the home of the Rowe family and of later owners of the works, while the left-hand half was used for offices for the works. The dividing wall between the two houses was not breached until 1952. After the soap works closed in the 1930s the buildings were used by Alfred Lockhart (Marine) and the houses became the administrative offices and caretaker's flat. In the 1950s the premises were bought by Varley Pumps & Engineering, later the Peerless Pump Company, and the houses went through more changes but were still used as offices. Peerless Pump finally left the site in 1989. The modern photograph shows the development of the area as part of the Ferry Quays estate of flats, shops and restaurants. The old house has been restored and it is still partly offices and partly residential.

*T*he entrance to Brentford Dock and the canal seen from the Kew bank of the Thames in the 1950s. In the 1850s the Great Western Railway Company purchased some low-lying land between the canal, the river Brent and the river Thames and their Engineer in Chief, Isambard Kingdom Brunel, designed a dock there, surrounded by railway sidings. It opened in 1859 with a railway line linking it to the main line at Southall. Heavy cargoes such as coal from the Welsh mines could be brought into the railway sidings in wagons and transferred to barges and thence down the Thames to London Docks. Imported goods and raw materials came in by barge and were then transferred onto the railway network for distribution round the country. As the Dock prospered more railway sidings and warehouses were built. A new wharf was opened along the bank of the Thames which meant that some boats did not need to come into the Dock to unload. The Dock closed in 1964 and the modern photograph shows that the warehouses have been replaced by the flats and houses of the Brentford Dock Estate, built in the 1970s.

A view of the Dock from just inside the flood gate when the site was being prepared for redevelopment in 1971. At its height the Dock handled huge amounts of cargo, imports of timber, steel and other raw materials, and exports of coal, chemicals, steel tubes and so on, but by the 1960s traffic was declining and the Dock was closed by British Railways in 1964. The site lay derelict for some years until the Greater London Council started to redevelop it as an estate of nearly 600 houses, flats and maisonettes built on the ex-railway land around the Dock basin. The first tenants moved into their new homes in 1977. The western end of the Dock basin was filled in and the remainder was kept as a marina with moorings for small boats. The modern photograph shows the same entrance wall and steps on the left, but the piece of machinery used to operate the flood gate is now just out of view. It has been turned on its side and is used as a base for planters of flowers. Some of the arches which supported the wharves have been retained as features in the modern development. The development was initially called the Tiber Estate, and each access road and block was named after a Roman ruler as tradition has it that Julius Caesar crossed the Thames at this spot. It is now known as the Brentford Dock Estate.

*T*he barge *Success* going upstream from Thames Lock in 1923. The *Success* was the first steel barge built by E.C. Jones (later E.C. Jones & Son), which had works just downstream of the lock on Brentside Wharf, now the premises of MSO Marine. The firm E.C. Jones was established in Brentford in the 1890s, first as a barge repairer and canal carrier and later as a boat builder. It was known for quality workmanship and built all kinds of boats including innovative 'Bantam' tugs that attached to the back of barges to push rather than pull. The Jones family sold the business in 1982, and it closed in 1992. When the canal was first opened from Brentford to Uxbridge in 1794 there was no lock here, but the tide caused problems for navigation so a lock was installed sometime before 1818. The building on the left beyond the lock is the engine house which contained the steam engines that provided power for the cranes used in Brentford Dock. The lower part of the brick wall of this building is still visible in the modern photograph just beyond the lock gate. In 1962 a second lock was added on the left and both were mechanised, and the lock keeper's house on the left bank was rebuilt.

The bridge over the canal just a little upstream from Thames Lock, *c.* 1900. The approaches to the bridge were gently sloped so that horses towing barges could easily walk over the bridge. By the time the bridge was altered to provide access to the Brentford Dock Estate in the 1970s, this was no longer a requirement and the current bridge has steps instead. Some of the industrial buildings on the right of the canal are still there 100 years later, including the premises of Band's Tannery near the bridge, which did not close until the 1980s. Some goods wagons on the railway sidings of Brentford Dock can be seen at the top of the bank on the left as the Dock was only just the other side of the embankment; in the modern photograph they have been replaced by the flats of the Brentford Dock Estate. The boats moored along the side of the canal in the old photograph were working boats, but those in the modern view are residential boats.

*L*ooking across the canal basin towards Durham Wharf and the backs of the houses in the High Street in the 1950s. This photograph was taken when the canal was still a busy commercial thoroughfare with barges laden with timber and other commodities continually passing through. Through the gap in the buildings the tower of St Lawrence's church can be seen rising above the other buildings. This tower, built of Kentish ragstone in the fifteenth century, is all that remains of the medieval church that once stood on this site. It was incorporated in the new church built in the 1760s, and is, in fact, the oldest building in Brentford. In the modern photograph the huddle of shabby industrial buildings along the side of the canal has been replaced by the new waterside flats of

the Brentford Lock development and a small area of natural wetlands on the right of the flats where water birds nest. Across the High Street two buildings survive to remind us of Brentford's past: St Lawrence's church and the Six Bells public house; the buildings in between them were cleared to make way for the access road for the Brentford Dock Estate.

A view of the canal basin looking towards Brentford Lock just after the Second World War. When the canal was opened in 1794 this lock was only a single one with a small stone hump-backed bridge just downstream from it, but in 1898 a severe flood damaged the bridge and the opportunity was taken to add an extra lock and replace the bridge with one providing more headroom. The lock was known as the gauging lock as this was where the cargo in each boat was gauged (i.e. measured) to assess how much toll had to be paid. Beside the lock to the right of the bridge the building with the steeply pitched roof and

decorative chimney pot in the middle is the toll house, built in 1911, where the clerk sat at a high desk to collect the tolls. The modern photograph shows that the sheds and piles of timber on the island have been replaced by new blocks of flats. At the time of writing there are suggestions that the toll house, which has been listed for preservation, could become an interpretative centre on the history of the canal.

*L*ooking up the canal towards the Great West Road in 1992 from the weir near the lock. This photograph shows some of the industrial buildings that lined the canal while it was still a busy commercial thoroughfare, although when it was taken commercial canal traffic had already ceased. The covered sheds that projected out over the water allowed cargoes to be loaded and unloaded from barges and narrow boats while being protected from the weather. On the left can be seen some of the industrial buildings on Commerce Road which was developed as the Brentford Factory Estate in the late 1930s. The modern photograph is taken from the same viewpoint but the industrial buildings on the right have been replaced by the blocks

of flats of the Brentford Lock development, recently completed. Pontoons have been built to provide moorings for pleasure boats and, appropriately enough, several narrow boats were berthed there at the time of writing. The structure in the distance to the right behind the trees is the headquarters building for GlaxoSmithKline on the Great West Road, completed in 2001.

The old mill on the western edge of the Butts, seen from the island looking across the river Brent, *c.* 1900; the houses in The Butts are just visible beyond the mill. There was probably a mill on this site from the mid-eighteenth century. By 1900 it had fallen into disrepair and was demolished to make way for a new building for the London City Mission's Boatmen's Institute. This was opened in 1904 and provided a base for the missionaries who ministered to the boat people as they stopped in Brentford to load and unload cargoes. There was a hall that could be used for services and for lessons for the boat children, and a maternity room for pregnant boat women. The Mission continued

to serve the boat people until commercial use of the canal ceased. It finally closed in 1978 and the building became a private house. The modern photograph shows the back of the Boatmen's Institute, and was taken from the same spot on the island which has now become part of the Brentford Lock development of houses and flats.

6

Gunnersbury Park

*A*t the beginning of the nineteenth century Gunnersbury consisted of two separate estates, each with a fine house and grounds. In 1835 the Rothschild family bought Gunnersbury Park, also known as the Large Mansion, and in 1889 also acquired Gunnersbury House (the Small Mansion). This photograph shows the Rothschild's household staff grouped outside the kitchens of the Large Mansion in 1914.

*T*he main entrance to Gunnersbury Park in Popes Lane, *c.* 1927. The men gathered at either side of the entrance gates are evidently hoping to sell refreshments to visitors; the cart on the left is labelled 'Pure Ices' and the bicycle is from a confectioner's shop. After the death of Leopold de Rothschild in 1917 some of the Gunnersbury Estate land was sold for building, and in 1925 the boroughs of Acton and Ealing bought the two houses and the remaining 186 acres of land. The grounds were opened as a public park in 1926 by Neville Chamberlain, then Minister for Health. Brentford and Chiswick Council became involved in 1927, and since 1965 the park has been financed and run jointly by the boroughs of Ealing and Hounslow. The modern photograph shows the same imposing entrance gates but the pond in the foreground is now entirely surrounded by railings and has become a nature reserve for water birds and plants. It is known as the Baron's Pond after Baron Lionel de Rothschild (1808–79).

Gunnersbury Park.

W 9084.

*T*he garden terrace of the Large Mansion in the early 1900s. This house, also known as Gunnersbury Park, was built by Alexander Copland, a partner in a building firm, in the early 1800s. It was bought by the financier Nathan de Rothschild in 1835. He died in 1836 but his architect, Sydney Smirke, continued to extend and remodel the house before Nathan's widow Hannah and the rest of the family moved in two years later. Over the next ninety years the Rothschild family enlarged and improved both the house and its grounds. They were great gardeners and encouraged the cultivation of rare and exotic flowers, fruit and trees. The terrace overlooking the gardens and the conservatory that the Rothschilds added at the eastern end of the terrace were always full of tubs of flowering plants. The modern photograph shows a more municipalised view – no flowers, just litter bins and park benches.

The drawing room in the Large Mansion in the early 1900s. In contrast to the rather plain exterior, Sydney Smirke's designs for the interior of the house were in a French-inspired neo-classical style with elaborate cornices, gilding and carved marble, making a sumptuous backdrop for the lavish entertainment hosted by the Rothschilds.

Guests who were entertained at Gunnersbury included foreign royalty and members of the aristocracy and of the Diplomatic Corps. After the estate was sold in the 1920s the Large Mansion took on a new role as a museum of local history. This began in 1929 when a public subscription was raised to buy the Sadler Collection of Acton material and since then the collections have been expanded to cover the boroughs of Ealing and Hounslow. The modern photograph shows the drawing room, now used to display the Rothschild carriages which are part of the museum's collection. The curved bay window and the decorated ceiling can still be seen and the heavily carved fireplace is partly concealed behind the carriages.

*T*he garden front of the Small Mansion in 1902. This house, also known as Gunnersbury House, was built by Stephen Cosser at around the same time as the Large Mansion, but the two estates, although physically so close, were entirely separate. They were not joined until 1889 when Leopold de Rothschild bought the Small Mansion to use as a guest annexe for the main house. In contrast with the more sober architecture of the Large Mansion the appearance of the Small Mansion was more lively, with a pierced roof balustrade decorated with urns, elaborate stucco window surrounds and an exotic oriental verandah decorated with bells. The wing containing the orangery with the tall chimneys and pepperpot turret was added later in the nineteenth century, probably by the Farmer family who bought the house in the 1830s. The modern photograph shows that most of the pierced parapets have been filled in and the orangery has been boarded up. However, the scaffolding indicates that remedial work is being carried out to the roof.

*T*he ruins of Princess Amelia's Bath House in the 1940s. The original Gunnersbury House, built in the seventeenth century, was owned by Princess Amelia, second daughter of King George II, from 1761 to her death in 1786. She spent £20,000 on repairs and improvements to the house and gardens. She added various buildings to the grounds, probably including this unusual little building to the east of the Small Mansion. It contains a grotto with a deep bathing pool; the walls are decorated with shells and shiny pieces of glass and flint to sparkle in candle light. There is a single chamber next to the grotto and at the back on the north side a small walled garden with a little cascade and a cave decorated with artificial stalactites, quartz crystals and fragments of alabaster. Sometime in the nineteenth century the Bath House was turned into a romantic gothic folly with pinnacles and mouldings. Unfortunately, by the time of the Second World War it had become a genuinely ruinous romantic folly. The modern photograph shows the Bath House after it had been restored from 2000–01 with the help of a grant from the Heritage Lottery Fund.

The Japanese Garden at Gunnersbury just north of the stable block, *c.* 1905. This garden, based on Japanese models, was created for Leopold de Rothschild and his wife Marie by their famous gardener James Hudson. There were winding streams crossed by narrow bamboo bridges, a Japanese style summer house, a wide variety of plants of Chinese or Japanese origin including bamboos and palms, and even two oriental stone lanterns. When the Japanese ambassador was invited to visit in 1905 he is said to have remarked, 'It is marvellous, we have nothing like it in Japan'. The garden survived until the Second World War, but then it could no longer be maintained and now all that is left are the concrete channels for the waterways and a few palm trees and other oriental trees and shrubs. An attempt to recreate the garden a few years ago failed through lack of funds.

Famous Old Gardens
JAPANESE GARDEN, GUNNERSBURY PARK.

ars outside the coach house in the stable yard, *c.* 1917. Leopold de Rothschild owned several successful race horses, but he was also interested in motor cars. This view shows the cars belonging to the Rothschild family with their uniformed chauffeurs drawn up in the stable yard. The stable block was built in 1836 to the design of Sydney Smirke, just south of the grounds of the Small Mansion. The owner of the Small Mansion objected to the stables and built a 'Gothic ruin' which can just be seen above the roof line to hide the view of the stable block from his gardens. The modern photograph, taken through the wire fencing which encloses the derelict buildings, shows a sorry sight. At the time of writing all efforts to find alternative uses for the stables which would allow the buildings to be repaired have been unsuccessful.

Great West Road

*T*he Great West Road looking west from the junction with Boston Manor Road in the late 1960s. The road was planned as a bypass for the increasingly congested Brentford High Street and was opened in 1925. The good communications and the ready availability of cheap land with plenty of room for building meant that the road was soon lined with large modern factories and became known as the 'Golden Mile'.

*T*he Great West Road looking east from the junction with Syon Lane in 1960. The building on the right with the tower was built for Brittol in the 1930s and was later used by the Admiralty Oil Laboratory. Next door is Coty's perfume and cosmetics factory, designed by Wallis, Gilbert & Partners in 1932. This closed in 1979 after the business was taken over by an American company. It was later used as offices, but was empty at the time of writing. The angular square buildings next door are the premises of Lincoln Cars & Leonard Williams which dealt in Packard cars from America. This is where a V2 rocket fell in March 1945, killing thirty-two people and destroying the factory. Beyond that the building with the taller central section is the fire extinguisher factory designed in 1929 by Wallis, Gilbert & Partners for Pyrene. The company remained here until 1969. Since then the building has been used as offices by several firms and in 2006 was occupied by Carillion. The façades of the Coty and Pyrene buildings are preserved by having been given Listed status and, as the modern view shows, they are the only survivors; the other factories in the photograph have been replaced by offices, industrial estates or large retail outlets.

*L*ooking west past the front of the Firestone factory in the mid-1960s, with the tower of the Gillette factory in the distance. Firestone's was one of the first factories to be built on the new road, making tyres to cater for the growing interest in motoring. It was designed by Wallis, Gilbert & Partners as the British branch of the Firestone Tyre & Rubber Company of Ohio and was opened in 1928. The works covered about 26 acres and by the 1930s was employing 1,500 people. It pioneered new designs in tyres for cars and for commercial vehicles of every kind but eventually was unable to compete with cheaper imported tyres and closed in 1979. The site was bought by a property company which surreptitiously brought in bulldozers to demolish the factory over the August Bank Holiday weekend of 1980 before the paperwork to preserve its outstanding Art Deco façade could be completed. The modern view shows the 1980s blocks housing The History Channel and PC World. These have replaced the Firestone building, but the railings with their distinctive pillars remain to show what was there before.

*T*he canalside premises of Trico-Folberth on the north side of the Great West Road, in 1991, the year the firm left Brentford. The founder of the American Trico company is said to have invented windscreen wipers after being involved in a motoring accident in wet weather because he could not see through the rain on his windscreen. A British subsidiary was set up in north London in 1928 to manufacture the windscreen wipers and moved to a new factory midway between Boston Manor Road and the Grand Union Canal in 1931. Later it took over the next door premises of Thompson & Norris' corrugated cardboard box factory which gave access to loading and unloading facilities on the bank of the canal. The works moved to South Wales in 1991, and the buildings were demolished in 1993. The modern photograph shows part of the new international headquarters building of GlaxoSmithKline which now occupies the site and which opened in 2001.

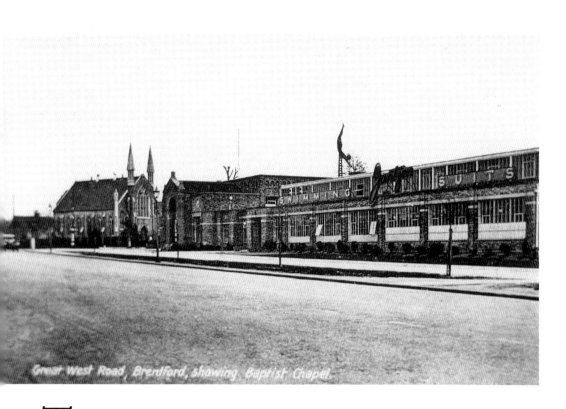

Great West Road, Brentford, showing Baptist Chapel.

*T*he south side of the Great West Road, looking east at the junction with Boston Manor Road, in the early 1930s. The building on the left with the twin turrets is Park Baptist church, erected in 1855 to seat 500 worshippers. It was demolished in 1990 after the dwindling congregation had merged with the United Reformed church at the southern end of Boston Manor Road. The other buildings are the premises of Jantzen Knitting Mills, built by an American swimwear manufacturer and opened in 1931. The buildings, with striking façades in orange-gold brickwork, were based on the design of the parent company's headquarters in America. The company's logo was a diving girl in a swimsuit, and a neon-lit version of this appears above the roof of the factory. The factory relocated to the West Country in 1962 and the buildings were demolished and replaced by Great West House, the recently refurbished office building seen in the modern view.

*L*ooking north up Boston Manor Road at its junction with the Great West Road in the 1950s. On the left is the factory built for Macleans in 1932. The company manufactured pharmaceuticals and toiletries. One of its most successful products was toothpaste, leading to the slogan, 'Did you Maclean your teeth today?'. The company was taken over by the Beecham Group in 1938 and ceased manufacturing on this site in the 1960s. In 1969 Rank Audio Visual took over the building for its marketing and service divisions, and converted part of

the factory into open plan offices. Rank moved out in the mid-1980s and the building stood empty for some years. It was eventually demolished in 1997. The modern view shows that the Macleans site is now part of the new headquarters building for GlaxoSmithKline. The big houses on the opposite side of Boston Manor Road have been replaced by another tall office block and by the elevated section of the M4, which was opened in 1965.

*T*he Great West Road looking east from near the junction with Ealing Road in 1962. On the south side of the road the tall central building with low flanking wings was designed by Wallis, Gilbert & Partners for Simmonds Aerocessories in 1937. The company made aircraft instruments and advertised its aeronautical connections with the sculpture of a pilot high up on the tower. After the war the building was taken over by the British Overseas Airways Corporation, and in 1955 it became the headquarters of the Beecham Group. Two of Beecham's best-known products, Lucozade and Brylcreem, are advertised on the façades of the buildings. SmithKline Beecham (as it had become after merging with SmithKline Beckman in 1989) merged with GlaxoWellcome in 2000 to become GlaxoSmithKline, whose new headquarters building is shown on the opposite page. The modern view shows how the elevated section of the M4 looms over the neighbouring buildings. Plans for redeveloping the Beecham factory site as a mixed site of flats, offices and shops are still under discussion at the time of writing.

*T*he east front of Carville Hall, in Carville Hall Park, in 1972. This early Victorian house was originally known as Clayponds, and its extensive grounds included the area of the park now on the north side of the Great West Road. The estate was bought by Middlesex County Council in 1918 as part of its plan to build a by-pass for Brentford High Street. Brentford Council bought the areas not required for building the Great West Road in 1922 with some of the funds raised to commemorate the dead of the First World War. It was opened as a public park the following year. The house was later converted into flats.

The building behind and to the left of the house is St George's School, built in 1893. In the modern photograph the house looks much the same as before, but the park is less maintained, and the sculpture of the lion has disappeared. The school, almost hidden behind the trees, has become a community centre. Just out of sight, but not out of earshot, the traffic on the elevated section of the M4 rumbles past.

*T*he premises of Smiths Crisps and Henlys Garage on the north side of the Great West Road, just east of the junction with Lionel Road, in the early 1950s. Smiths Crisps first opened a single-storey factory here in 1927, but the business grew so quickly that by 1930 this had been replaced by a two-storey factory with 3 acres of floor space and a handsome colonnaded front. Smiths left in 1970 and the buildings were later used by Strand Glass, and demolished in 1988. Henlys, once the UK's biggest motor agency, opened a car showroom and service station here in 1936. Its premises were designed by Wallis, Gilbert & Partners and boasted a round-topped clock tower and a graceful curved canopy which arched over the petrol pumps along the whole length of the façade. In the late 1950s the building became a distribution depot for Martini but it was taken over by Fiat in 1978 so reverted to its original function as a car showroom. After a disastrous fire in 1989 the tower had to be rebuilt but, as the modern photograph shows, it is still a landmark although somewhat dwarfed by the tall office blocks on either side. It is now the headquarters of EMC2.

Other local titles published by Tempus

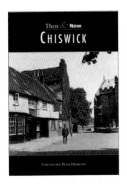

Chiswick Then & Now
CAROLYN AND PETER HAMMOND

This fascinating volume takes a selection of historic photographs, the majority of which have never before been published, and matches each one with a modern view of the same location. Accompanied by descriptive and informative text, each pair of images charts the history of Chiswick and highlights some of the major changes to streets, shops and local industries which have taken place over the last century.

0 7524 3062 9

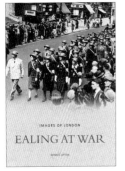

Ealing at War
DENNIS UPTON

Published on the sixtieth anniversary of the end of the Second World War, in association with the Ealing Library and Information Service, *Ealing at War* offers a unique record of the wartime history of the people of Ealing, Acton and Southall. Illustrated with 100 archive photographs and documents, the book recalls life on the Home Front, drawing on the first-hand accounts of those who were present during those dangerous years.

0 7524 3518 3

Haunted Wandsworth
JAMES CLARK

From heart-stopping accounts of apparitions, manifestations and related supernatural phenomena to first-hand encounters with French poltergeists and prison spectres, this collection of stories contains both well-known and hitherto unpublished tales of the ghosts, mysteries and legends of Battersea, Balham, Putney, Tooting and Wandsworth.

0 7524 4070 5

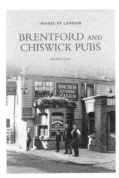

Brentford and Chiswick Pubs
GILLIAN CLEGG

Brentford and Chiswick lie on the River Thames and the main route to the west of England, so pubs sprung up to provide succour for travellers and workers. Illustrated with nearly 200 archive images, *Brentford and Chiswick Pubs* captures over 100 pubs and breweries and gives details of their dates, their whereabouts and their history.

0 7524 3723 2

If you are interested in purchasing other books published by Tempus, or in case you have difficulty finding any Tempus books in your local bookshop, you can also place orders directly through our website

www.tempus-publishing.com